ULTIMATE GUIDE TO IMPROVING ORGANISATIONAL CHANGE READINESS

Learn how to manage a sustainable change processes and how your company will react to change

Ifra Publication

CONTENTS

WHAT YOU'LL LEARN

1. Understand the need for change, and how people respond to it
2. Establish a corresponding procedure that will help them to make informed decisions
3. Master strategic thinking
4. Successfully implement change

ABOUT

S kills for managing change are not only necessary if you want to remain relevant in a world where it is the norm. Ultimate Guide to Improving Organisational Change Readiness is a Book that will teach you how to protect your career from risk.

You'll first investigate a more individualised strategy that enables you to pinpoint your personal motivations for change, making it simpler to maintain drive and concentration. After that, you'll find a framework that addresses both the attitude and the useful/ actionable aspects of the situation.

The team dynamics component of transition preparation will also be covered. After completing this Book, you'll be equipped with the information, abilities, and practical measures necessary to change the status quo in your field and succeed in a dynamic environment.

WHO THIS BOOK IS FOR

1. Senior managers
2. Strategists
3. Business owners who need to reposition
4. Representatives of new business startups that are considering entering a market

INTRODUCTION

Hello, everyone. My name is Ifra, and welcome to my Book, Ultimate Guide to Improving Organisational Change Readiness. After doing marketing and consulting for close to 15 years now, I can vouch for the fact that there is no skill more important, more vital, than your ability to change and adapt to new circumstances. The main purpose of this Book is to instil in you the mindset and philosophy that will allow you to deal with any unforeseen problems and challenges, to give you the tools and resources to take advantage of new opportunities and do so with a minimum of resistance, be it internal or external.

And here's how we're going to tackle this. We'll first identify your own unique why, your motives to adopt change and also help you better define it. After we get this out of the way, we'll look at dealing with adversity and change resistance, meeting head-on the main challenge in your pursuit of change readiness. Afterwards, we don't waste any time and jump right to the actual framework to develop your change readiness skills. And instead of addressing them individually, we look at things in what I consider a far more effective approach.

The main objective is for you to take action, and that happens at the intersection of three things: your desire, your want to do it; your knowledge, your what to do; and your skill, your how to do it. We cover all of them in detail, with a strong focus on your own unique scenario. So be prepared for quite a few exercises, where you'll have to think things through in order to get the most value out of the Book. And then we also address the team dynamic of change readiness because, let's face it, you won't be doing this alone.

Solid and healthy communication and collaboration are paramount. And my personal promise to you is that by the end of this Book, you'll have a clear and actionable framework that will allow you to not only effectively react to problems and challenges, but also become a driving force of change in your organisation, in your industry, and in your own life. I hope you'll join me on this journey of developing your change readiness skills here on Amazon.

DEFINING CHANGE AND IDENTIFYING YOUR MOTIVES TO ADOPT IT

D efining change and identifying your motives to adopt it. Hello, my name is Ifra, and you're reading Ultimate Guide to Improving Organisational Change Readiness. And it seems that now more than ever, change is becoming the norm, not something you do once in a while. So why do we need to change, and why is it such a difficult undertaking? And the truth is, we're creatures of habit.

We like our little routines, good or bad. They give us a sense of control over our lives. And change is the exact opposite, lack of control, lack of predictability, chaos. And we tame that chaos by taking on responsibility. The more projects we manage, the more perceived control we have over the world around us. But what we often forget is that chaos and order, change and stability, are interdependent. You could look at it philosophically with the yin and yang symbols, where the two halves are chaos and order, and you will see that inside each one you have the seed for the other. But you can also look at it from a pragmatic perspective and realise that most successes started from chaos. So when it comes to change, you're either the one creating it or the one reacting to it.

We enact change in moments of inspiration or in moments of desperation, and we all know which one is more common. And that's probably the reason we avoid change so much. That's why we fear it. So in the first two chapters we'll be focusing on mindset and framing the problem, so please be patient while we go over this part, because if we get this right, taking action will be the easy part. Friedrich Nietzsche famously said, "He who has a reason to live can bear almost any how." And that's what we want to achieve in this first chapter: identify your reasons to change. So let's begin.

Look, I'm not going to bore you with the obvious statement that your skills need to be constantly refreshed. You already know that, and you can easily validate this statement by looking at yourself and the people around you. Those that are successful are in one of two categories. Either they have become highly efficient and specialised in their field, or they constantly changed and adapted, and many of them never imagined in their wildest dreams that they would be doing what they currently are 3 or 5 years ago.

The main problem with change is that refusing to play the game is not an option. Imagine you stop learning for 3 or 5 years. How easily can your work be replaced by a script, a robot, or even an actual person that can do things twice as fast or at half the price? So as the first exercise, I want you to do this. Get out a piece of paper, yes, an actual piece of paper, and split it in half with a vertical line. On the left side, write what you think would happen if you stopped changing entirely for the next 3 years. Is your current job obsolete? Is your organisation even relevant anymore? Is it the one disrupting, or is it the one that will be disrupted? What about the industry as a whole? Does it still exist? And now comes the second part.

On the right side, write what you think your life would be if you changed the norm, if you automated part of your own work and focused on bigger goals, if you started to really optimise everything. How will things be if you took charge? And to help you out, I'll share with you what I wrote. From the moment I started to have a decent level of success, my biggest fear, my archnemesis, as I like to picture him, was a 16-year-old kid who lives with his parents that has the drive and eagerness to work 10, 12, 14 hours a day, that realised that there's no secret to success. So he works all hours of the day because he has no bills to pay, no short-term earnings goal, no other responsibilities or commitments.

How fast can he get to where I am? And whenever I feel the distance between me and that kid is getting too close for comfort, I get motivated and step up my game. On the other side, for me, there's the thrill of exploration, of satisfying my curious nature. Five years ago, I never dreamed online Books would make up most of my income. So who knows what to expect from the next 5 years? Not knowing what comes next but being optimistic about it is a great feeling. So before moving on, please pause this video and do this exercise.

Left side, your life with no change, right side, your life focused on change and optimization. And as we go through the Book, I want you to always have this somewhere in sight. This will be your reason for moving forward, and it should scare you and inspire you at the same time. And for those of you that want a more in-depth approach to this, I recommend you enrol in Jordan Peterson's Self Authoring program. At the time of this recording, it costs just $30. And, oh, Professor Peterson might be considered controversial by some, but in my opinion, the Self Authoring program is a very well structured and formalised way of establishing where you started from, where you are, and where you want to be.

And putting this in words has a huge impact on your results moving forward. And now that we've clarified your why, it's time to look at better defining change. I'm looking forward to seeing you in the next video.

DEFINING CHANGE

Defining change. So what has changed for you? As we discussed earlier, change starts from a state of inspiration or desperation. Yet embracing change should be methodical. It should be a process. That's why I recommend you look at it in the framework of risk/reward. So before moving forward, you should first define your goal. What is it that you think should change in your career? What is it that you're aiming for? What change would offer the biggest benefit to you?

It can be a step towards a management position or a lateral move, or simply getting better at what you currently do. And as with most decisions, you already know what needs to be done. Quite often we seek counsel for validation more than we do for insight. I remember the story told by Steven Covey, author of The Seven Habits of Highly Effective People, where a student asked him how he was doing in his class. Stephen calmly looked at the boy and replied, well, how are you doing? And at that moment, the student realised that what he wanted the answer to was not how he was doing, but rather to find out if the teacher had figured it out. And realising his true goal was not to hack the system, he replied, well, I haven't really applied myself lately.

I could do better, and in fact I will do better. Another great way to decide what to change is by using the Pareto principle. It states that 80% of your results come from 20% of your work. Focus on the important 20%. Or the other way around, focus on optimising the ineffective 80% of your work and have more time for the important few. And once you've set your objectives comes the most important part. Identify the metrics you'll use to keep track of your progress. There are countless studies that show that the mere act of tracking your weight helps you lose a few extra pounds each year, so never ignore the impact of simply measuring your efforts. You can do it with time spent on that activity, budget, by creating milestones.

Depending on what works for you, track things daily or on a weekly basis. The idea is to have something with small enough increments so you see your progress and stay motivated, yet big enough so they are not trivial. And after you've clarified your why, your objectives, and how to keep track of your progress, it's time we move on to the biggest challenge in execution: change resistance and paying the cost of change. I'm looking forward to seeing you in the next video.

CHANGE RESISTANCE
AND THE COST
OF CHANGE

C hange Resistance and the Cost of Change. This is by far the biggest problem you will face, dealing with adversity, external, and change resistance, internal. However, before diving into the core of this chapter, I'd like to discuss framing, and, more precisely, we'll discuss your perception and what role it plays in the context of change readiness. There's this great example you can read in the book Release Your Brakes by James Newman about a girl that got to hate spinach, although she never ate any.

One evening, she was at a friend's house, and her friend's Mom asked if she'd stay for dinner. Her friend immediately said that she'd better go because they're having spinach, and it's horrible. So she left. Several days later, her own mother asked her dad if he wanted spinach for supper, and he politely declined. Then one day when her mother cooked spinach again, her little girl refused to eat it, saying she hated spinach. When her mother insisted, saying she never had any. How can she possibly know if spinach is good or bad? She refused even harder, and everything turned into a fiery argument with the conclusion that eating spinach is pure torture, and all her knowledge was based on partial or incomplete maps of reality.

Maybe her father refused spinach that evening because he had some in the morning. Maybe she has completely different dietary preferences than her friend. Maybe her friend's mother used a different recipe when cooking spinach. Maybe she would have enjoyed it. But when forced to eat it, she linked so much pain and anger to it, thus making spinach unbearable. And this example is quite easy to follow. More often than not, our perception of people, events, and circumstances is in the same way flawed because it's based on incomplete or inaccurate maps of reality. So you might be wondering, what does this have to do with change readiness?

And the answer is simple. Your perception of an event changes everything, so it's very important that it's accurate. If you use flawed data, your results will never be valid. With that in mind, I recommend before every meeting, before every important call, or especially before sending out that furious email, always pause for a moment, breathe, and take another look at the situation. Is your understanding of it accurate? Is there something you are not aware of? Is there any insight you are lacking?

Don't make decisions based on beliefs. Try to make them as much as possible based on facts. And speaking of decisions, that's what we're going to cover next, taking ownership, one of the best ways to take on change and also an effective ingredient to change resistance. I'm looking forward to seeing you in the next video.

TAKING OWNERSHIP

T aking ownership. There is no greater challenge when dealing with change than your own internal change resistance. As the saying goes, you are your own worst enemy, and that is why you need to start taking complete ownership for your actions. When you fail, don't blame it on external factors. It's on you. The data shows that when you are proactive and are the one taking on the challenge with its innate risks, the odds of success are greatly increased in comparison to when things happen to you. So how do you go about this?

How do you take action? And the best framework I know is your circle of influence. You focus on the things you can control. And the more you do this, the more your circle of influence grows, and the circumstances where you can make a change will grow as well. If you don't take responsibility for your shortcomings, for your own failures, this circle will never grow because it's never your fault. It's always external factors. And you place the power of change outside yourself. You can't have it both ways. You can't have growth without taking on more responsibility.

And the first step is to start asking better questions. So let's say you want to improve your team's productivity and decide that a daily report system would help. However, although everyone agreed to your idea, nobody actually completes their report at the end of the day. A justified, yet highly ineffective question will be to say to yourself, why are these people so lazy? What is wrong with them? Yet by doing so, you're doing what we've just discussed. You are blaming external factors.

A far better question would be what can I do to get them to complete that daily report? Or what can I do to understand the reason for not completing that report? So once again, the best place to start when taking ownership is by asking questions that empower you. Then, focus on things you can act on. And coming up next, we're going to look at another big part of change resistance, escaping your autopilot. I'm looking forward to seeing you in the next video.

ESCAPING YOUR AUTOPILOT

Escaping Autopilot. And the easiest way to think about this is with a thermostat in mind. Either consciously or subconsciously, we want things to stay the same. The bad part about this internal thermostat is that it works both ways. When you are unsatisfied with your current results, you will change in order to get back to your default. However, when your current results are above your default, you will start behaving in such a way to lower it, even if that implies self-sabotage. So you can easily see that adopting a culture of change readiness is in conflict with this internal thermostat.

It's actually interesting that something that is strenuous for us is second nature to the way we create AIs, which, let's face it, are the pinnacle of effectiveness. Not sure if you know of OpenAI, a company backed by Elon Musk, that's focused on developing AI technology. In a past event, OpenAI made a bot for the game Dota 2. Dota is a competitive multiplayer game where teams of five battle each other, controlling herpes with a wide variety of trades and skills. The level of complexity is enormous with players needing hundreds of hours just to become familiar with the game, and most professional players have over 10,000 hours of playtime.

The initial bot OpenAI created was for a simplified version of Dota, a 1v1 matchup. And what makes it relevant to our example is how it learns. The bot plays against itself. And if it wins, that version becomes the new default. And it keeps testing and growing with these small increments, starting with nothing more but the basic game objectives as input. The main advantage it has over human players is the fact that it can simulate tens of thousands of hours of gameplay in a few days. And as expected, it managed to beat all professional players that it played against during the event.

It was only a few months later that a player called Black managed to beat it, and one commentator immediately pointed out how short-lived this success will be, stating Black is the new OpenAI now because as soon as the match ended, the strategy to defeat it immediately became obsolete. And this is the moral of my story here. Your approach to change should not be to just change once, but make change the norm. As soon as a successful iteration is made, you need to make it your default and start working on the next one. And all this comes at the cost, and knowing that cost is the starting point towards escaping your autopilot. So coming up next, we have Identifying the Cost of Change.

IDENTIFYING THE COST OF CHANGE

Identifying the Cost of Change. So far, we've clarified the importance of having an accurate perception, taking ownership, and how to escape your autopilot. All have the role to reduce change resistance and make dealing with adversity easier. Yet you will always have to pay the cost for change, and that cost is risk, risk of failure, risk of losing face, risk of wasting resources like time or money. There's always something you are putting on the line, and it's your role to identify if the gamble is worth it or not. And the difficult part is not knowing what you are risking. That's easy.

The difficult part is being comfortable with making that decision because the level of risk is specific to who you are. There is no right or wrong here. People are succeeding across the entire spectrum. Take the stock market, for example. At one end of the continuum, you have extremely successful day traders. And at the other end, you have Warren Buffett who makes a move once every few weeks or months. It's really a matter of what works for you and learning as you go. So how do you find that sweet spot for risk without having to make a lot of uncomfortable and bad decisions?

I got my risk management insights from real-time strategy games. Other people got it from playing poker. Some learned it from playing sports. And I'm sure you have in your own life a hobby, a special interest, that has given you priceless insight on when to make a move, went to wait, went to be aggressive, and went to fall back.

Use that seemingly unrelated insight to identify your risk aversion. You'll discover that when you strip those scenarios of context, the process is the same. And that was all on change resistance. Coming up next, we have the core chapter, Developing Your Change Readiness Skills. So I'm looking forward to seeing you there.

DEVELOPING YOUR CHANGE READINESS

Developing your change readiness skills. As we discussed earlier, change happens in one of two cases, you either create it or you react to it. However, like most things in life and business, it's not always a black and white scenario. It's more of a gradient between initiation and reaction. And on this axis, you have skills that are more or less effective based on the type of event. For example, being proactive and being a quick starter are obviously more important when you want to implement a new idea.

Skills like being able to focus are useful in both cases. And then you have skills like being a fast learner and making accurate decisions under stress, which are of far greater importance when reacting to change. And let's not forget the group-level ones like being an effective communicator and leader. Now I could go on and talk about each individual skill on this list. Yet, I think a far more important approach is one where we have taken action at the centre because, in essence, that is the end game for changing readiness, to effectively act or react.

So our approach moving forward will start from here, the intersection of your desire, your want to do it, your knowledge, your what to do, and your skill, your how to do it. So let's start with desire, you want to do it. We've already clarified your why and defined what to change. That is why, in this video, I'd like to focus more on the practical side of what you want to do, the part where you go from idea to execution, which is actually a trade specific to all successful people. And this is a growing problem due to an exponential rise in access to resources and information. We can learn almost any skill we want. Yet, we limit the experience to learning alone.

And instead of learning being a means to an end, it has become the goal, and there's nothing wrong with being more knowledgeable. In fact, it's far better than ignorance, but we miss out on so much potential. Learning is safe. Doing exposes you to failure, and that's the problem with learning. It has no or little inherent risk. That's why you must focus on doing and not delay with more information gathering, more research, more learning. And one of my aims with this Book is to help you minimise the inherent risk of doing so you pull the trigger. And the main cause for hesitation is fear, fear of losing face, fear of failure or even fear of success.

Because if you win, you have to keep doing it. What will other people think? Did you just get lucky the first time? So that's what we're going to look at next, fear, and more precisely, running towards it, not from it. I'm looking forward to seeing you in the next video.

GO TO WHERE
THE FEAR IS

G o to Where the Fear Is. We've already talked about the discomfort change creates and how you deal with change resistance. Fear is the last obstacle in your pursuit for change. The bigger your goals, the more discomfort, anxiety, and fear you have to deal with. It's normal. However, I want to remind you that it is in those states of mind that progress happens. Growth never comes from comfort. Growth comes from struggle, frustration, and the desire to improve.

And the moment you realise that fear is actually an indicator, you're on the right path, not a stop sign. Your relationship with it changes, and you can use that to your advantage. Not sure how many of you saw the recent Netflix series The Last Dance. I think we can all agree that the name Michael Jordan is synonymous with performance, competitiveness, and overcoming impossible challenges. And you saw how hard it is to keep going after you've won everything there is to win.

And I distinctly remember several moments throughout the series where Michael created those scenarios in his own head where people were disrespectful to him in order to get fired up and motivated. These made-up stories touch on the exact problem we are discussing in this first part of the framework, creating and growing your desire, your want to because desire is the hard part, especially after you've achieved a certain level of success. And considering you're reading a Book on change readiness, it's almost certain that you have achieved that plateau.

Skills and knowledge simply take time to acquire, but wanting to is the hard part. And there's a big difference in how you do things if you have to versus doing them because you want to. But enough with the philosophy. How do you go about this? What can you do to make yourself take more action? And strategy number 1 is to create a narrative to motivate yourself. You've already started in the first chapter with visualising your life 3 years from now with and without change. Maybe with your newly gained insight, work more on those stories.

Make them even more personal. Strategy number 2 comes from author Jordan Peterson. It's actually one of his 12 rules for life. It's to take care of yourself as if you are taking care of someone else you are responsible for. It's easy to be driven and optimistic on your good days. But what do you do when you have bad ones? How do you go about that? Well, this is the way. You treat yourself as if you're someone you are taking care of. You stop being your own jailer. You should maybe give yourself a break.

You stop blaming yourself. And even if this makes you move slower towards your goal, it prevents the biggest risk, giving up. And that's what we're going to look at next. How do you keep doing it? How do you stay focused? I'm looking forward to seeing you in the next video.

STAYING FOCUSED

Staying focused. Probably the simplest way to see how effective this is to success is with the marathon example. If you ever ran in a marathon, you always saw that group of people who run fast at the start and get a significant lead, only to be overtaken after 2 or 3 miles by more experienced runners that kept a steady pace. It's easy to stay focused for a few days after reading this Book, yet the real success comes from making all the small changes consistently over time.

And one of the main reasons why people are not consistent is far more dangerous than fear or anxiety. It's boring. It's complacency. You simply lose interest. That intense emotion you had at the beginning is gone, and with it the drive to follow through. I remember this interesting quote from a football coach that said, a good coach is not one that gets you going when you want to. That's easy. It's one that gets you going when you don't want to. So how do you do it? How do you keep going day after day? And here are some ideas to start with. Can I encourage you to explore creating your own based on what you know motivates you?

Woody Allen famously said, 80% of success is showing up. So goal number one is to get to work and start doing. Look, I have trouble being productive just as the next guy. And if you've read any of my Books, you know that I stay focused using the Pomodoro technique. You know, work 25 minutes uninterrupted, then take a

5-minute break. I actually do a modified version of this, focusing for anywhere between 40 to 90 minutes without interruption, and then I take a 20-minute break. The reason for this is because my challenge is getting started, not staying focused. I always struggle to get myself to start a Pomodoro, so I promise myself that I can take a break any time after just 10 minutes.

Yet I have to focus on those 10 minutes. And guess what? In 90% of cases, I end up working for as long as 2 hours without any interruptions. But maybe your problem is not getting started. Maybe your problem is with the constant interruptions from your team. In that case, you might suggest something like silent timeslots, where nobody interrupts each other. You could start with a timeframe of just 2 or 3 hours a day and see where it goes. Or maybe the problem is your bad habit of checking social media every 15 minutes. In that case, the solution might be a browser extension that blocks access to specific sites.

And with the risk of repeating myself, you know best what's stopping you from staying focused, and all you have to do is take action and make those changes so you can focus. And that was it on the desired part of the change readiness framework. Moving on, we're going to look at knowledge. I'm looking forward to seeing you in the next video.

KNOWLEDGE: YOUR WHAT TO DO

K nowledge: Your What to Do. And it's only natural we start with a quick look at decision making and cognitive biases and make sure our decision-making process is reliable and valid. All decisions are linked to four interdependent criteria, outcomes, choices, timeframe, and involvement. Making a decision sooner might give you more choices. Involvement of less parties might speed up the execution, yet it might negatively influence outcomes.

And considering you never have infinite time or data to make the perfect choice, you're always taking a calculated risk. The traditional model of decision making has the following steps. First, you prepare for the decision by gathering data. The only risk at this stage is to fall into the trap of paralysis by analysis. Then, comes making the actual decision, which is the simplest part. As Nike puts it, you just do it. And you follow it by communicating the decision to those influenced by it. And this stage boils down to three things, what the decision was, who made it, and why was it made.

And the last step is as important as making the decision itself. You have to set up in place a feedback loop that monitors if the outcome is the one aimed for and adjust Book if needed.

And as you can see, there's no rocket science level of complexity here. So you might wonder why there are so many bad decisions being made every day? And that leads us to our next topic, the biggest threat to decision making besides bad data, and these are cognitive biases, mistakes in our reasoning where we hold onto beliefs and preferences despite existing contrary information.

We're all wired to have cognitive biases, and even when we are aware of them, we're still vulnerable. And I'll briefly go over a few of the most common ones, and probably the most frequent one is confirmation bias where you have a tendency to search for data and interpret it in such a way that it validates your existing beliefs. Then, you have the anchoring effect where we rely too much of our decision on a single fact usually discovered at the beginning of our search. You then have the bandwagon effect. You no longer invest in thorough research because most of the group already agrees on something.

Another common one is the gambler's fallacy where you think that future probabilities are influenced by past events. If you flip the coin 10 times, and it was heads the 11th time, the odds are still 50/50. They don't change. They are separate events. And there are hundreds more biases that negatively impact our decision making, and you can never truly escape their influence.

The only measure to counter cognitive biases is to constantly ask yourself how objective is the data you are making the decision on? Is it something you want to believe or is the decision based on fact? Are you mistaking correlation for causation? Are you searching for a pattern where there is none? And I think now you're ready for the five core strategies for change readiness, which we'll cover in the following video. I'm looking forward to seeing you there.

CORE STRATEGIES FOR CHANGE READINESS

Core strategies for change readiness, and these are by far the most effective methods when it comes to either creating change or adapting to it. If you want a more in-depth coverage, I recommend you give my other Book, How to Stay Abreast in the Ever-changing World of Tech a listen. It complements this one focusing extensively on the how-to part of keeping your skills sharp in any field. But for now, let's proceed. First strategy is to always move your feet. The idea is simple.

Small, consistent progress is always better than no progress. What do you think the hare and tortoise fable is all about? The principle of slow and steady wins the race is timeless because it's innate to us as humans. People that are consistent have been the ones more likely to succeed. So as a practical exercise, take a look at your current goals, even those you made in the past and failed to achieve and adapt them based on this new approach. Moving forward, we have the second strategy, solving a problem, and for me personally, this is the most impactful one. Whenever you want to learn a new skill, improve your service, or disrupt an industry, you need to solve a problem.

I remember an old interview with Jeff Bezos where he shared his focus with Amazon. I'm paraphrasing here, but he said something in the lines of people will never complain about getting the product faster or at a better price, so we focus as much as possible on those two things. You should have a similar mindset. What are the most important things you can change? Moving on from solving a problem, our next core strategy comes to fix a problem traditional education created. It states that there is no speed limit. Let me clarify. Most of our learning experience, in fact, almost all of it was in a group setting.

While group learning has many benefits, when it comes to rapid acquisition of skill, individual learning is much faster. The main problem with group learning is that speed is changed so everyone can follow. When you are learning on your own like reading this Book, you are doing things at your own pace, and based on your familiarity with the topics, you can go faster or slower. You can skip things you already master and focus on those that are new. And you can also improve that speed in other ways by prioritising interests by reducing distractions and also by working on your perception of the topic.

It's a given fact that we learn the things we enjoy faster. So the concept to remember here is not to learn at the speed that is expected of you. Learn at the fastest speed you can. And our next strategy is probably the most effective way to achieve any skill. Get yourself a mentor. Find someone who already is where you want to be in the future and mimic their behaviour to shorten your path to success with their insight. And the last strategy is the mirrored version of this one. You should teach. Nothing clarifies concepts and gives you a deeper understanding of topics than teaching them.

Explaining to others makes you look at a problem from all angles. You discover aspects you never considered. I personally know no expert in any field that doesn't allocate some time to sharing their wisdom with others, and I can't say if they do it for a sense of contribution or just because they enjoy doing it, but the fact alone that all of them are doing it points to it as a core strategy towards staying sharp and being at the top of your game. And the last ingredient for all these core strategies is constant supervised stress. You heard the famous saying that it takes 10,000 hours to become a master at something. Well, that timeframe has been both greatly over and under estimated at the same time.

Exaggerated because you can achieve mastery in far less time and underestimated because it's not enough to put in those hours, you have to spend them under constant supervised stress. You need to have a clear objective when spending them. I created hundreds of Google Adwords campaigns. By doing hundreds of campaigns the same way does not grant me expertise, but testing out thousands of ads does, always trying to improve my click-through rate, my conversion rates, my ad quality score, the landing pages that I send traffic to, looking for keywords that cost less and convert better.

Constantly striving to improve my metrics is what makes me a proficient Google Adwords campaign manager, not the hours I've spent alone. And you can think about these core strategies similar to aiming a gun. A one-degree shift in aim has a huge impact on where you hit the target. And now we'll move on to the third and last component of developing your change readiness skill, the how to do it. I'm looking forward to seeing you in the next video.

SKILL: YOUR HOW TO DO IT

S kill, your how-to-do-it is part of developing your change readiness. The reality of the matter is that in this department, it's still you who knows best. As I said at the beginning of the Book, quite often the problem with change and adapting to it is not that you don't know how to proceed, but rather that you don't have the willpower, the mindset, the resources, or the right habits to do so. That leaves only two things that I can help out with in the skill department.

It's how to speed up your learning and how to stay up to date and relevant in what you do. You'll notice that some of the things we'll discuss overlap with the strategies previously mentioned, and that is because learning is an emotional experience. The more intense and positive the emotion linked to that new skill, the easier it is to learn it. As Plato famously said, learning should never be forced. It should be a voluntary experience. With that in mind, here are some practices you can use to accelerate the speed at which you acquire new skills. One of the most effective approaches is to have a mindset of play.

Especially when getting familiar with a new concept, play is a strategy that will reduce that initial struggle of learning something from scratch. So look at learning a new skill as an experiment. This way, you are replacing failure with discovery. Then comes something I talked about in a previous chapter, your perception. If you link too much pain to learning a new skill, you will simply avoid it. That is why you need to condition yourself to associate something positive to it, explore all the benefits and add more weight to the positive side. The next practice is one that not only helps with learning but also helps boost your team's synergy. It's cooperation, learning in a group setting and utilising each other's strengths and covering for each other's weaknesses. However, always make sure to have the end goal in mind and not waste time and energy keeping track of each member's contribution, because that can easily turn into a political game.

And here's one that we all need more of. Do not neglect sleep and rest. It is fundamental in the formation of long-term memory. And like with everything in life you care about, you need to make time for learning. Look, we're all busy. We all have that other project, that other client, the other thing we need to do first. If you don't set aside time for learning in your day, just as you would for a client or a project, you will never do it. And that was it for accelerating your learning. Moving on, we have updates and networking, and we'll start with updates, the news-like the component of staying up to speed.

The main issue with news is that it's not actually learning, and that makes it liable to become procrastination and not a productivity enhancer. That's why you should remember this easy-to-follow checklist. Step number 1, set up Google Alerts for the topics you are interested in professionally. Make sure to make your alerts as specific as possible so you don't get bombarded with generic information that you will end up ignoring. Step number 2, identify and follow industry influencers, both individuals and companies. This should take just a few minutes each day or each week and will prove immensely helpful in staying up to date with trends and changes and even open the door for career opportunities. Step number 3, contribute.

Try putting something out there. Think of it like your public notebook, where you share thoughts, predictions, concerns, tools. This is one of those activities that has the immediate benefit of helping you better define your thoughts but can also have a tremendous impact long term by opening up new opportunities and deals that otherwise would have never been possible. I know several such stories of people who got overnight job offers after their organisation went belly up, or of successful collaborations and friendships that started from a Facebook conversation with a stranger.

And speaking of friendships, we have networking, the last part we're going to address in this chapter, and it's an area of business that has been hit the hardest in the COVID era. And while in the past, offline events were far more frequent, now the focus will have to shift more to virtual, but the principles stay the same. Look, we all know that even live events rarely if ever bought us that groundbreaking insight they sold us on. But it was that small chat you had with a stranger after the keynote, the question someone from the audience asked that made you look at things differently. Meeting new people is the wildcard in business. You never know who you're going to meet and how that is going to change your career. So try as much as possible to be a part of the community.

However, as with updates where procrastination was a risk, in the case of online networking, the main risk is starting fired-up conversations. Sharing insight and ideas can rapidly turn into you defending your ideas and focusing on proving the other person wrong. And while with friends who know you this is never a problem, when it comes to strangers, people don't always know you have good intentions at heart. So you might end up proving you're right, but how will that help you? So make sure to always remember that the goal is learning and sharing knowledge, not validating existing ideas, not creating your very own echo chamber, and not winning debates. And that was it on the framework for developing change readiness.

I tried to have a balance between structure and freeform, sharing action lists side by side with best practices in the hopes to increase the odds of you integrating as much as possible from the Book into your workflow. So if there's any topic you want additional material on or want further ideas for implementation, don't hesitate to reach out to me. I'll be happy to help. Coming up next, we have changed readiness in a team setting, because, let's be honest, you won't be dealing with this alone. I'm looking forward to seeing you in the next chapter.

CHANGE READINESS
IN A TEAM SETTING

C hange Readiness in a Team Setting. Up until now, the Book focused exclusively on you, the individual. However, it's quite obvious that change doesn't happen in a void. There always is a group dynamic to it, and change readiness in a team is primarily dependent on two factors, communication and collaboration. And this chapter aims to focus on the principles and actions fundamental to those two factors. So, here is how we're going to tackle this. We'll first look at the essential principles for effective communication. We'll look at trust, clarity, speed, and simplicity.

We then move on to your communication channels and format, basically shifting focus from principles to purpose and function. And last, we'll take a close look at the fine details of effective communication. More precisely, how to find balance between chasing performance, yet maintaining a healthy organisational culture. So without further ado, let's proceed. Fundamental principles of effective communication and collaboration, and these are trust, clarity, speed, and simplicity. And your role is to find the right mix of the four. And one specific aspect of this system is that those fundamental principles are quite often mutually exclusive. On many occasions, you will have to trade one for the other.

It's quite obvious that communicating faster can damage clarity, thus leading to misunderstandings and errors. The same can be said about trust. A low trust level in your organisation leads to all the briefs and meetings taking longer and being more detailed. So long story short is that you cannot have it all. You always have to compromise based on your immediate and long-term goals. The good thing is that the better you understand these principles, the less you lose in the trade off of one for the other. So let's begin. There is one principle that you can never have too much of, and that is trust. Yet what makes trust different from all the others is that it takes time. Trust requires real work.

It can't be hacked. There's no quick fix to it. To gain it, you simply have to be a trustworthy person. You make good on your promises, allocate time to understanding others, and make changes based on their feedback, and you do this consistently over time and your trust account will keep growing. And the beauty of it is that at some point you will fail. You will be disappointed. Yet you will still have people's trust if your deposits were consistent over time. And it doesn't stop here, it also helps with our next principle, clarity. When trust is high, you don't need to invest as much in making your communication clear. And if I were to summarise the problem most organisations have when it comes to clarity, it would be with this quote by George Bernard Shaw.

"The biggest problem in communication is the illusion that it has taken place." We quite often fail to remember that the role of communication is so the other person understands us, and that implies that we, the emitter of the idea, are also responsible for the receiver deciphering the information. So you might say, okay, make sure the other person understands me. Well, in fact, it's the other way around. In order to maximise clarity and communicate effectively, your focus should be first on understanding the other person, then making yourself understood. And you can easily spot this flaw when having a fired-up argument.

Quite often, we fail to listen, and while the other person speaks, the main thing on our mind is what we'll reply with. So once again, make sure you first understand, then proceed with making yourself understood. Next on our list, we have speed. You can't say productivity without speed. We're always searching for a faster way to achieve our goals, to grow, to maximise output. And there is no intrinsic problem with speed, yet it is a root cause for many of the problems we face. Speed increases the number of errors your work has. Speed might lower trust because you don't make time to listen.

Speed makes you compromise on safety, yet at the same time it is the pressure that makes us act. Speed is to communicate what risk is change management. It's that dial that you have to constantly operate and adjust to maximise performance. And our next and last communication principle has the role to help you with just that, how to operate that dial with the minimum trade off. I'm talking about simplicity, and it's obvious that the more complex a process, the higher the chances of miscommunication. It's also self-evident that simple ideas are those that stand the test of time. That's why we have inspirational quotes and not inspirational novels because they give a huge insight in a compact form. So your focus should be to always look for ways to simplify, say more with less, cut rules and guidelines, eliminate unnecessary meetings, calls, and try to make your organisation leaner.

If you want to be ready for change, make it easy. Simplify. And that was it on principles. Coming up next, we're going to look at communication channels and format. I'm looking forward to seeing you in the next video.

COMMUNICATION FORMAT AND CHANNELS

Communication format and channels. Look, as we already clarified, effective communication and collaboration are essential to change readiness in a team setting because the faster and clearer you communicate with your team and partners, the sooner they will be on board with the change in vision and execution. That's one of the main reasons why small teams are better at reacting to change. But it's not the size of the organisation alone. It's also the strength of the interpersonal bonds inside that team.

Trust is high, communication is fast, thus decision making is better, and this leads to a better response to change. And you can look at communication format and channels as the infrastructure for boosting your team's change readiness. You first have the goals and objectives point of view. Here, you can identify the role communication plays. It can be to cooperate, to track progress, make decisions, get or offer feedback, and learn. Knowing the objective changes how you approach things. For example, if you're having a meeting to make a decision due to a recent industry change, then the goal is to react fast and have reliable data to base your decision on.

If you're giving feedback to a new employee, obviously, your approach should be different. While in the first scenario you would be objective and firm, in the latter, a calm, reassuring, and patient approach would yield far better results. So you can see that having the objective in mind makes a big difference to your effectiveness. That's why I strongly encourage you to pause this video, take out a piece of paper or open up a new document, and write up a short summary of your day focusing on your communication activities. You might have a list that starts with a short update meeting in the morning, calls with clients, suppliers, partners, offering feedback and guidance to a junior on your team. Then maybe a team meeting focusing on quarterly goals. Then maybe having a tough discussion where you bring to the attention of someone that you are not satisfied with their results.

And now comes the interesting part. Based on the objective of each of those activities, write down what you think you can do differently to make that communication more effective. And this leads us to another criteria of structuring your communication, and it's based on how big of an impact that type of communication will have. So, for example, on one end of the continuum, you have company updates with minimal impact on day-to-day activities, and those could easily be handled with a quick email or a post on the company message board.

However, when the change is significant, like firing someone, then you need to become much more personal, going for a phone call or a face-to-face meeting. And although those personal talks could be more difficult and even unpleasant, you might lose empathy, but you will never lose respect for having them. And at the end of the day, respect is essential to trust going beyond your likability. And before moving on to the last part of this chapter, I'd like to properly address the communication segment where most organisations fail and miss out on enormous potential, and that is feedback. Giving and receiving feedback is the same as trust. It takes time, it takes work, and there is no overnight fix to it. There are two main problems when implementing feedback systems.

The first one is that feedback, the most transformative type, is negative. You learn and grow when you find out you are wrong. And you might have guessed that we don't like being told we're wrong, even if we know we are. We have this limbic response when we get bad feedback. We feel as if we're under attack and respond immediately. While in the jungle 10,000 years ago that would have helped, when we're working together on a project, this instinct does more harm than good because we place ego and politics ahead of our communication objectives. And the only solution here is to retrain yourself and your team with constant reassurances that negative feedback is not about the person, but about the work.

I remember a physics teacher from high school. When you get an F, it doesn't mean you're an F student, and that's your label for life. It simply states that on that test on that day, that was your skill level. That has nothing to do with your potential with how you would fare on the next test or next year, and you should always remember that. So try and integrate this philosophy into your organisational culture. It will make dealing with negative feedback and moments of crisis much easier and also reduce tension and personal grudges. The second problem with feedback systems is that they are a maintenance-heavy operation. You don't only have to implement them, also monitor and take action based on the feedback you receive.

If, let's say, you go for the popular idea of having a suggestion box where everyone can give input, if you never make a change in the Book of a year or never read those suggestions, it will actually do more harm than good. People will ask themselves, what's the point when being asked for feedback in all future efforts? So remember that follow-up, whenever implementing a feedback system, is the most important part. And now we'll take a close look at how to navigate the realm of maximising performance while fostering a healthy organisational culture. I'm looking forward to seeing you in the next video.

ORGANISATIONAL CULTURE AND PERFORMANCE

Organisational culture and performance. And here's why this is so important. On one side you have culture, which is all about how you do things, who you are as an organisation, as a team, as individuals. And on the other side you have performance, which is all about results, metrics, and data. And these two will come into a hard conflict at some point. That's what we plan on achieving with this video, how to navigate through difficult decisions when you will pick one for the other.

What will you decide when it makes more sense to fire a third of your organisation because you automated an entire process? Your allegiance is to the organisation and its efficiency. But at the same time, those people are your team and friends, and they have always been loyal to the firm and literally did nothing wrong. And the truth here is there is no right or wrong choice. You simply make a decision and live with the consequences. And I'll share two stories from two completely different people that will hopefully help you with all the hard decisions when it comes to change. First one is from Jack Welch, the former CEO of General Electric, a man who many claim is the best CEO of the century.

And he talks about firing an engineer who was doing really poorly. And while getting fired might seem like a bad moment in everyone's career, that engineer started working with another organisation where he thrived and eventually ended up competing with General Electric. The cruel thing would have been not to fire him and tell him he was doing a good job, although the work was subpar. Then, when a serious crisis would have occurred, he would have been fired. At that point, he would have been years into his profession, being lied to all this time that the work he delivered was good. In this case, being fired is a much bigger setback. So you can see that not all good news has good outcomes nor bad news bad outcomes, as you'll discover in the next story as well.

I've heard this one from an Alan Watts lecture. For those of you who don't know who Alan Watts is or what he does, he's a British philosopher from the 60s who interpreted and popularised Buddhism, Zen, and Eastern philosophy. The story goes like this. Once upon a time, there was a Chinese farmer whose horse ran away. That evening, all his neighbours came around to commiserate. They said, we're so sorry to hear your horse has run away. This is most unfortunate. The farmer said, maybe. The next day, the horse came back bringing seven wild horses with it. And that evening, everybody came back and said, oh, isn't that lucky, what a great turn of events, you now have eight horses. The farmer again said, maybe. The following day his son tried to tame one of the horses, and while riding it he was thrown and broke his leg. The neighbours then said, oh dear, that's too bad. And the farmer responded, maybe.

The next day the conscription officers came around to conscript people into the army, and they rejected his son because he had a broken leg. Again, all the neighbours came around and said, isn't that great? Again, he said, maybe. In essence, you never know what will be the consequence of misfortune, and you never know what will be the consequence of good fortune. That's the beauty of change. Coming up next we have our final chapter where I have compiled all the action points I've mentioned throughout the Book in an easy-to-follow guide and also share the further reading list in case you want to pursue a specific topic. I'm looking forward to seeing you there.

IMPLEMENTATION GUIDE AND FURTHER READING

Implementation Guide and Further Reading. First of all, I want to congratulate you for reaching the last chapter of the Book. It shows a lot of commitment on your part, but it also shows that you're the kind of person that likes to see things to completion. Many studies show that fewer than one in four people read a book in the past year. If you look at online Books' completion rates, you will also see that a high percentage of people don't even read them from start to finish, let alone take action on what they learned. So before we proceed with the implementation guide, I want you to realise you are among the very few that take improving themselves seriously.

Yet, that realisation should not make you complacent and comfortable. It should come as a responsibility you take onto yourself to not only learn but also take action. Knowledge is always an improvement to one's life, but applying what you know is where significant change takes place. So let's begin. We started out by clarifying your Why. Why change? Having clear motives makes a huge difference in those moments of self-doubt, of low morale, when you are on the brink of giving up. So I recommend you take out a piece of paper, split it in half, and on the right side, write about your life three or five years from now if you've stopped changing, stopped adapting, stopped learning. And on the other side, your career if you made change the norm, if you constantly sought out self-improvement.

So now you identified a reason to change. What comes next is the What? What exactly should you change? And the simplest yet most effective way of identifying what to focus on is by using the Pareto principle. What work gives you the highest return on investment? And now that you clarified the Why and the How regarding change, it's time to look at the challenges of change readiness, and these are dealing with adversity and your internal change resistance. And the first step in dealing with both is to make sure you have an accurate picture of the problem, and the first step towards fixing the discrepancies between our map and the territory is to be aware of this very fact: The map is not the territory.

Moving on, we discussed the practice of taking ownership and how being proactive towards change boosts the likelihood of success. And the best starting point was to ask better questions, questions that empower you, that focus on the things you can change and have control over and not blame external circumstances or other people. Failed a job interview? Don't re-affirm in your head how bad you are at interviewing. The damage is already done. Ask yourself, How can I avoid making the same mistakes next time? Then deliver a project on time.

Late for a meeting? Don't ask, Why am I so bad at managing my time? Ask, Okay, my time management skills are not what I want them to be. What can I do to improve this? Moving forward, we looked at your internal thermostat and why you should fight it and adopt change as a lifestyle, not just something you do in times of crisis. And, of course, we addressed the elephant in the room--the cost of change, which in essence is risk, risk of failure, losing face, wasting resources, and there is no manual on the ideal level of risk. It all depends on your own risk aversion. Some people have incredible results with high risk/high reward strategies, while others perform better playing it safe.

I recommend you look for other areas in your life where you already actively play with risk, be it a sport, a game, a hobby, and use that insight in your career. Quite often, we compartmentalise our skills and fail to benefit from using them to improve different areas of our lives as well. We then focused on the core framework for change readiness where, instead of talking about each skill in isolation, we looked at things starting with the main objective, having the ability to act or react effectively to change. And this happens at the intersection of desire, your want to do, knowledge, your what to do, and skill, your how to do. With regards to desire, we already clarified your Why earlier in the Book, so the only thing that was left was actually doing. And the most frequent cause for not doing is fear, and that is why we allocated an entire video to your relationship with fear. A good place to start is to look at how real those perceived risks really are, and you'll discover that the risk is greatly exaggerated. Even more so, you need to look at fear as an indicator you are moving in the right direction. And a good place to start and overcome those negative emotions is to remind yourself why you're doing what you're doing.

Always bring back focus to your Why. And I'm realistic about this. We're not all Michael Jordan and have superhuman levels of determination. You will reach a point where you will want to give up. And for that scenario, an effective approach to keep yourself going is to take care of yourself as you are taking care of someone else you're responsible for. We then moved on to the knowledge component where we looked at the five core strategies to maximise your change readiness. The first one was to move your feet and focus on doing, actually pulling the trigger on your plans, not just thinking about it. The second strategy is to have the mindset of solving a problem. This approach makes your objectives clear, measurable, and less restrictive when it comes to methods. So if you currently have a vague goal of learning a new language or to get proficient at something, try to change it to something more specific.

What exactly do you want to achieve with that skill? And the next strategy is to acknowledge the self-limiting belief that you have to move at a certain pace. A pattern started in school where everyone learned at a medium pace that was too slow for some or too fast for others, depending on the subject. Once you realise how much of your potential is limited by your own beliefs, you'll be amazed by how fast you can really go, especially with regards to change. And the last two strategies are interlinked. They are to get a mentor and to teach.

And the secret ingredient that is fundamental to the What to do part of change readiness is constant, supervised stress, a form of pressure that keeps you on track. Think of it like the force that's meant to balance out comfort and complacency. And what's left is skill, the How to do it part of our framework. And in this department, you are once again the expert. You know the specific how-to's. All that I can do here is to help you more easily acquire new skills and set up a system for staying up to date. In the case of skill acquisition, things are pretty simple. You need to actively make time for it. Otherwise, it will never happen.

Try to have a fixed time slot during the week with a clear objective on what you will learn. And with regards to staying up to date, here is a three-step process that applies to almost any field and requires minimal effort. Step number 1: Set up Google Alerts for the topics you are interested in. Make tweaks so you don't get bombarded with too much genetic information. Step number 2: Identify and follow industry influencers and make sure to allocate at least 20 or 30 minutes each week to get up to speed with everything they share. Step number 3: Contribute. It's highly important that you don't stay just a consumer of news.

Try putting something out there. It can be your own thoughts on tools, industry changes, and predictions. You never know how you might grow a following, stand out from the crowd, or simply contribute to moving the industry, even if by a small margin, but in the direction you want it to move. If you never make your voice heard, your chances of making a change are zero. At least by sharing your thoughts, there is one, and one is always bigger than zero. And that was it for changing readiness at the individual level. Yet we don't live in a void, do we? We're all part of teams which we rely on, and that is why you also need skills that are specific to a team setting. And we first addressed the four principles that will improve your change readiness as a team: Trust the foundation to all successful communication, and what you have to do here is take a moment, look at the current relationships with each member of your team and see how you can boost trust.

Maybe in some cases, an overdue apology or explanation is in order. Maybe a word of encouragement. Maybe a serious talk with someone who has been neglecting their responsibilities. After trust, we have clarity, which counterintuitively is achieved by making a real effort to understand the other person, then making yourself understood. Up next, we have speed, which acts like the counterweight to the initial two. Speed can be an advantage, but it can also be the reason for miscommunication, low quality of work, and conflict. And our last principle comes as a catalyst to all of your communication efforts. It is simple.

Nothing makes you more prepared for change than this. Having simple-to-follow processes and procedures reduces errors and makes dealing with crises manageable. That is why I highly encourage you to take a moment if you haven't already and do an audit of all your current workflows and focus on reducing or altogether removing the dead weight. Maybe you don't need 2-hour-long meetings, and 30 minutes are enough. Maybe you don't need a 10-point guideline, and 5 is enough. Maybe some reports could be simpler. And remember when communicating with your team to make sure to use the appropriate channels.

As a rule of thumb, the bigger the change you want to communicate, the more personal the interaction should be, despite it being more difficult. And the last topic we've covered was finding the right balance between culture and performance, a tough one because there is no right or wrong answer here, just as there is no right or wrong answer when you will be faced with difficult decisions that will change the lives of others. And my only advice here is to be true to yourself. In my country, we have a saying: "Man sanctifies the land," referring to the fact that you have the power to change the world around you based on your own actions and beliefs. However, you're not the only one making changes. Thus, the need for change readiness, having the skills to react to threats, and also take advantage of new opportunities that arise. And that was it.

Coming up next, I've prepared a list of additional resources that you can use to further deepen your understanding of various topics I've covered throughout the Book, everything from decision making to taking ownership, willpower, flow, choice, and even organisational culture. I'm looking forward to seeing you in the next and final video.

FURTHER READING

Further Reading. And I'd like to start with something that is much more than a book. As the author himself says, this is not a book of the month that you read and forget. You can think of it like a life manual, and I constantly find myself coming back to it. I'm talking about "The 7 Habits of Highly Effective People." Whenever you're in doubt with your why's and your aim in life, I recommend you give this book a read. Moving on, we have "Release Your Brakes" by James Newman. And you can look at this one like a manual for your brain.

It will help you better understand the way you operate and how to have a more accurate map of reality. Up next, we have "Rework" by Jason Fried, a book that is very practical in nature. You can get from it huge insights on how to look at work, how to boost your productivity, and also how to be the initiator of change and not just react to it. Still in the practicality section, we have Cal Newport's "Deep Work" that for me that wonders in the sense that it's more of a manual for knowledge work. And since you're on Amazon, I'm going to go out on a limb here and presume most of your work is in front of a computer, most of it requires a lot of brain time, and this book deals with maximising this type of work. Moving on, we have another classic in the area of focus, "Flow" by Mihaly Csikszentmihalyi.

In many ways, the same topic as the previous one, just a different perspective. Then we have "The Power of Habit" by Charles Duhigg, a manual for habit creation. Another book that will do wonders for those of you who, like me, suffer from chronic paralysis by analysis is "The Paradox of Choice" by Barry Schwartz. It will help you make decisions faster, better, and with far less second guessing yourself. If you're not sold, I at least encourage you to watch his TED talk. Another one that actually inspired the way I structure my Books with all the practical exercises intertwined with the content is "The Willpower Instinct" by Kelly McGonigal. It's a very practical and actionable resource to increase your willpower, and I advise you to at least read a summary.

You'll spend 10 minutes, but you will get so many powerful insights. And we've reached the last category of books, the autobiographies section, and the reason I find this category important is because they work as a mentoring program. You get raw practical advice from people that have been there and done that, and you get more than just the polished version. If you read Elon's biography by Ashlee Vance, you'll learn about the struggles SpaceX faced at the beginning, and the very out-of-the-box solutions they used. You'll also learn that his office language is not that PR-friendly, and I think knowing the bad parts, the struggles these people we admire face, will help us deal with similar struggles.

One biography in particular I recommend is "Delivering Happiness" by the late Tony Hsieh. The reason is because a big part of the book focuses on something I recommended you do as well, more precisely, use the insight you have from one area in your life in other areas. In the case of Tony, you'll learn about his passion for poker and how he used that experience in business. So, long story short, read up on the people you aspire to, but not just the PR material that's being made pretty and appealing. Read up on the challenges, the problems, the cost they paid for their success. And one last resource that will surely help you to adapt to change is a website called ProductHunt.

It's basically a directory of tools that serve almost any need. So, either you're looking for a project management app or a tool to automate part of your work. If it exists, you will find it here. And that was it. My name is Ifra, and you have readed Ultimate Guide to Improving Organisational Change Readiness. It's been a real pleasure creating this Book for you, and I hope you enjoyed reading it at least half as much as I enjoyed making it for you. I want to thank you for your attention, for your commitment to improving yourself, and I'm eager to hear your thoughts and the results you got from applying what you've learned in this Book.

And if there's anything you need my help with, I am at your service, and it will be my pleasure to contribute to your individual and team's success. In the meantime, I wish you good luck in all your efforts, and remember that what makes knowledge powerful is taking action!

Printed in Great Britain
by Amazon